YOUR KNOWLEDGE HAS VALUE

- We will publish your bachelor's and master's thesis, essays and papers

- Your own eBook and book - sold worldwide in all relevant shops

- Earn money with each sale

Upload your text at www.GRIN.com and publish for free

Stanko Radmilovic

Household final consumption. Rank positions in a sample of 55 countries (and 11 indicators)

GRIN Verlag

Bibliografische Information der Deutschen Nationalbibliothek:

Die Deutsche Bibliothek verzeichnet diese Publikation in der Deutschen National-
bibliografie; detaillierte bibliografische Daten sind im Internet über http://dnb.d-
nb.de/ abrufbar.

Dieses Werk sowie alle darin enthaltenen einzelnen Beiträge und Abbildungen
sind urheberrechtlich geschützt. Jede Verwertung, die nicht ausdrücklich vom
Urheberrechtsschutz zugelassen ist, bedarf der vorherigen Zustimmung des Verla-
ges. Das gilt insbesondere für Vervielfältigungen, Bearbeitungen, Übersetzungen,
Mikroverfilmungen, Auswertungen durch Datenbanken und für die Einspeicherung
und Verarbeitung in elektronische Systeme. Alle Rechte, auch die des auszugsweisen
Nachdrucks, der fotomechanischen Wiedergabe (einschließlich Mikrokopie) sowie
der Auswertung durch Datenbanken oder ähnliche Einrichtungen, vorbehalten.

Imprint:

Copyright © 2013 GRIN Verlag GmbH
Druck und Bindung: Books on Demand GmbH, Norderstedt Germany
ISBN: 978-3-656-59222-8

This book at GRIN:

http://www.grin.com/en/e-book/267537/household-final-consumption-rank-positions-
in-a-sample-of-55-countries

GRIN - Your knowledge has value

Der GRIN Verlag publiziert seit 1998 wissenschaftliche Arbeiten von Studenten, Hochschullehrern und anderen Akademikern als eBook und gedrucktes Buch. Die Verlagswebsite www.grin.com ist die ideale Plattform zur Veröffentlichung von Hausarbeiten, Abschlussarbeiten, wissenschaftlichen Aufsätzen, Dissertationen und Fachbüchern.

Visit us on the internet:

http://www.grin.com/

http://www.facebook.com/grincom

http://www.twitter.com/grin_com

Job 0001103690

BOOKS

Prof. dr Stanko Radmilovic, Novi Sad, Serbia

Household final consumption - Rank positions in a sample of 55 countries (and 11 indicators)

Short substantive references to the "Household final consumption expenditure, etc.." and without wider elaboration article in its entirety

Macroeconomic category "Household final consumption expenditure, etc.." essentially (and in simplified terms) is part of GDP, which is (in one way or another) extracted from the real sector of the economy. It is clear that he does not spend the whole finally and promptly. The reasons are both economic and technical, and here we can not go into detailed explanation. There is important to highlight two other important implications: (1) This means that the gross domestic savings (accumulation) is not only the primary form of retained profits in the real economy (in microeconomic entities), but also (2) that extracted portion of GDP (the part that is not consumed promptly) outside the sector of the real economy, secondarily formed (included in) the gross domestic savings (accumulation). This opens up the possibility, moreover, necessity of known traditional function of time (term), space and special purpose transformation part of GDP extracted from the real sector of economy.

In the time before the financial liberalization and financial globalization (ie at the time was not yet discarded Bretton Woods arangement and it incorporated Keynesian stance: 'Let goods be homespun whenever it is reasonably and conveniently possible; and, above all, let finance be primarily national.'") - thus formed savings "returned" to the economy, through the domestic banking sector, primarily by financing of real domestic investment.

Later, after a financial revolution, and now too - not only in countries with highly developed and globalized financial systems, than in countries with underdeveloped financial systems and the domination of foreign banks in the domestic banking sector - domestic savings flows, formed outside of the real sector of the economy, often go completely different. It's here can not consider wider.

But at least it should be said that in countries with performances much like the Serbian economy, the dominant foreign banking entities (both objective and subjective reasons) that part of the gross domestic saving too little (if at all possible to talk about the relevant part) directed to fixed domestic investment and much more redirected to the household sector for financing final consumption, mostly foreign goods.

Household final consumption - Rank positions in a sample of 55 countries (and 11 indicators)

Data source for making / processing of these indicators and explanation of the categories in a call. 3-13, see the foot of the table

		GDP growth (annual %)	Agricul., value added (% of GDP)	Industry, value added (% of GDP)	Servic., etc., value added (% of GDP)	General govern. final consum. Expend. (annual % growth)	Househ. final consum. Expend, etc. (% of GDP)	Gross capital format. (% of GDP)	External balance on goods and servic. (% of GDP)	Capital Coeffic. (I 2000-10 / (GDP 2001-11)	Gross domes. savings (in % of GDP)	FDI, net inflows (in % of GDP)
1	2	3	4	5	6	7	8	9	10	11	12	13
1	Moldova	5,1	18,3	17,7	64,0	7,0	91,6	27,3	-37,2	1,8	-9,9	6,2
2	B - H	4,0	9,4	25,5	65,0		91,4	21,8	-37,3	2,2	-15,4	4,6
3	Albania	5,2	22,7	19,1	58,2	5,3	87,9	26,2	-23,3	2,6	2,9	6,1
4	Montene.	3,6	10,6	21,7	67,7		79,2	23,6	-27,2	2,2	-3,6	
5	Macedon.	2,8	11,8	29,5	58,7	1,1	76,2	23,0	-18,7	2,2	4,3	5,4
6	Serbia	3,7	12,8	28,4	58,7	6,8	79,1	21,1	-20,3	1,8	0,8	3,9
7	Romania	3,9	10,5	37,1	52,4	7,0	71,2	24,5	-8,0	1,9	16,5	4,6
8	U S	1,8	1,2	21,7	77,2	2,0	70,3	18,0	-4,4	4,7	13,6	1,7
9	Greece	1,5				2,1	70,6	22,9	-11,9	3,4	11,0	0,8
10	Turkey	4,6	10,1	28,5	61,5	3,9	70,6	19,5	-2,9	1,6	16,6	1,7
11	Bulgaria	4,1	8,3	29,3	62,3	2,1	67,1	25,7	-10,6	2,3	15,1	12,3
12	Mexico	2,4	3,9	33,0	63,2	1,1	66,3	24,0	-1,7	3,8	22,4	2,8
13	Cyprus	2,8	3,0	19,2	77,8	3,3	65,7	19,5	-3,4	2,3	14,8	7,4
14	Lithuania	4,6	4,6	30,9	64,5	3,0	64,9	21,5	-6,4	2,0	15,1	3,6
15	Portugal	0,7	2,9	25,3	71,8	1,5	64,7	23,3	-8,3	3,7	15,0	3,5
16	U K	1,9	0,8	23,7	75,4	2,1	64,5	16,7	-2,3	3,6	14,4	5,0
17	Poland	4,0	4,4	30,8	64,8	3,9	63,4	21,2	-2,4	2,2	18,5	3,9
18	Latvia	4,4	4,0	22,4	73,6	-0,2	62,6	29,4	-10,9	2,8	18,5	4,3
19	Argentina	4,5	8,9	32,3	58,8		61,9	19,5	5,3	2,8	24,9	2,2
20	So. Afric.	3,5	3,1	31,6	65,3	4,6	61,8	18,5	0,2	1,5	18,6	1,7
21	Brazil	3,6	6,0	28,0	66,1	2,9	61,0	17,9	1,0	1,1	18,9	2,9
22	U. A. Emir.	4,9	1,5	52,9	45,6	5,7	60,8	21,7	10,0	1,6	31,7	3,6
23	Indones.	5,3	14,6	46,3	39,1	7,6	60,7	26,3	4,8	1,4	31,1	0,7
24	India	7,2	19,4	27,3	53,3	5,9	59,5	32,2	-3,0	2,3	29,1	1,6
25	Italy	0,7	2,3	26,9	70,8	1,4	59,5	20,8	-0,1	3,4	20,7	1,1
26	Croatia	2,5	5,5	27,9	66,7	1,2	59,4	25,3	-5,1	3,0	20,3	5,2
27	Ukraine	4,7	11,1	34,0	55,0	1,7	59,4	22,1	-0,4	1,7	21,7	4,3
28	Switzerland	1,9		26,3		1,0	59,0	21,6	8,1	2,2	29,7	5,0
29	Japan	0,8	1,3	28,4	70,3	1,9	58,1	22,3	1,0	6,0	23,3	0,2
30	Spain	2,2	3,4	28,6	68,0	4,3	58,0	27,0	-3,6	3,5	23,4	3,8
31	Germany	1,3	1,0	29,3	69,7	1,2	57,9	18,5	4,6	2,9	23,2	2,0
32	Slovak R.	4,4	4,2	36,3	59,5	3,8	57,6	26,1	-2,9	2,5	23,2	4,7
33	France	1,4	2,4	21,1	76,5	1,6	57,0	19,9	-0,6	2,9	19,3	2,7
34	Israel	3,8				2,1	56,8	18,1	-0,5	2,4	17,6	4,1

35	Australia	3,0	3,1	24,3	72,6	2,9	56,8	26,6	-1,0	1,9	25,7	3,2
36	Canada	2,2	2,0	31,9	66,1	2,8	56,3	21,4	2,4	2,4	23,8	3,5
37	Hunga.	2,2	4,4	30,4	65,2	1,2	55,5	23,1	0,3	2,6	23,3	11,5
38	Belarus	7,1	10,5	41,1	48,5	0,9	55,4	31,0	-5,4	2,7	25,6	2,4
39	Slovenia	2,7	2,7	34,1	63,2	3,1	55,1	26,3	-0,6	3,4	25,7	2,3
40	Estonia	4,7	3,7	28,4	67,9	2,5	54,8	29,9	-3,5	2,7	26,5	9,9
41	Austria	1,8	1,8	29,6	68,7	1,2	54,5	22,8	4,0	3,0	26,8	5,0
42	Korea, R.	4,5	3,4	37,4	59,2	4,2	54,3	29,5	2,1	3,8	31,6	0,6
43	Venezue.	3,5	4,5	51,9	43,6	6,4	52,9	24,0	10,8	2,6	34,8	1,3
44	Belgium	1,6	1,0	24,2	74,9	1,7	52,3	21,4	3,4	2,9	24,8	16,4
45	Finland	2,2	3,0	32,4	64,7	1,2	51,9	20,5	5,1	2,9	25,6	3,6
46	Czech R.	3,4	2,9	36,1	61,1	1,6	50,3	27,3	1,4	2,5	28,8	5,3
47	Russian F.	5,3	5,2	35,8	59,0	1,5	49,4	21,7	11,3	1,3	33,0	2,5
48	Denmark	0,9	1,7	25,0	73,3	1,5	48,2	20,2	4,8	3,0	25,0	3,3
49	Sweden	2,5	1,8	27,5	70,7	1,0	48,2	18,4	7,0	2,2	25,4	4,7
50	Netherl.	1,6	2,2	24,4	73,4	2,9	47,8	19,7	7,4	2,9	27,0	6,0
51	Ireland	2,9	1,9	36,2	61,9	2,9	47,0	21,4	14,4	3,7	35,8	15,0
52	Norway	1,7	1,6	40,9	57,6	2,4	43,0	21,6	14,6	2,2	36,3	3,0
53	China	10,2	12,0	46,5	41,5	9,3	38,8	42,5	4,5	2,2	47,0	3,6
54	Sa. Arab.	3,7	3,4	54,3	34,0	8,6	32,4	20,4	23,7	1,7	44,1	3,4
55	Qatar	13,1					15,6	33,5	30,6	1,6	64,1	3,8

Izvor podataka za izradu/obradu ovih indikatora: WB DataBank, maj 2013

Objašnjenje kategorija u kol. 3 - 13:

GDP growth (annual %) (Col. 3): Annual percentage growth rate of GDP at market prices based on constant local currency. Aggregates are based on constant 2000 U.S. dollars. GDP is the sum of gross value added by all resident producers in the economy plus any product taxes and minus any subsidies not included in the value of the products. It is calculated without making deductions for depreciation of fabricated assets or for depletion and degradation of natural resources.

Agriculture, value added (% of GDP) (Col. 4): Agriculture corresponds to ISIC divisions 1-5 and includes forestry, hunting, and fishing, as well as cultivation of crops and livestock production. Value added is the net output of a sector after adding up all outputs and subtracting intermediate inputs. It is calculated without making deductions for depreciation of fabricated assets or depletion and degradation of natural resources. The origin of value added is determined by the International Standard Industrial Classification (ISIC), revision 3. Note: For VAB countries, gross value added at factor cost is used as the denominator.

Industry, value added (% of GDP) (Col. 5): Industry corresponds to ISIC divisions 10-45 and includes manufacturing (ISIC divisions 15-37). It comprises value added in mining, manufacturing (also reported as a separate subgroup), construction, electricity, water, and gas. Value added is the net output of a sector after adding up all outputs and subtracting intermediate inputs. It is calculated without making deductions for depreciation of fabricated assets or depletion and degradation of natural resources. The origin of value added is determined by the International Standard Industrial Classification (ISIC), revision 3. Note: For VAB countries, gross value added at factor cost is used as the denominator.

Services, etc., value added (% of GDP) (Col. 6): Services correspond to ISIC divisions 50-99 and they include value added in wholesale and retail trade (including hotels and restaurants), transport, and government, financial, professional, and personal services such as education, health care, and real estate services. Also included are imputed bank service charges, import duties, and any statistical discrepancies noted by national compilers as well as discrepancies arising from rescaling. Value added is the net output of a sector after adding up all outputs and subtracting intermediate inputs. It is calculated without making deductions for depreciation of fabricated assets or depletion and degradation of natural resources. The industrial origin of value added is determined by the International Standard Industrial Classification (ISIC), revision 3. Note: For VAB countries, gross value added at factor cost is used as the denominator.

General government final consumption expenditure (annual % growth) (Col. 7): Annual percentage growth of general government final consumption expenditure based on constant local currency. Aggregates are based on constant 2000 U.S.

dollars. General government final consumption expenditure (general government consumption) includes all government current expenditures for purchases of goods and services (including compensation of employees). It also includes most expenditures on national defense and security, but excludes government military expenditures that are part of government capital formation.

Household final consumption expenditure, etc. (% of GDP) (Col. 8): Household final consumption expenditure (formerly private consumption) is the market value of all goods and services, including durable products (such as cars, washing machines, and home computers), purchased by households. It excludes purchases of dwellings but includes imputed rent for owner-occupied dwellings. It also includes payments and fees to governments to obtain permits and licenses. Here, household consumption expenditure includes the expenditures of nonprofit institutions serving households, even when reported separately by the country. This item also includes any statistical discrepancy in the use of resources relative to the supply of resources.

Gross capital formation (% of GDP) (Col. 9): Gross capital formation (formerly gross domestic investment) consists of outlays on additions to the fixed assets of the economy plus net changes in the level of inventories. Fixed assets include land improvements (fences, ditches, drains, and so on); plant, machinery, and equipment purchases; and the construction of roads, railways, and the like, including schools, offices, hospitals, private residential dwellings, and commercial and industrial buildings. Inventories are stocks of goods held by firms to meet temporary or unexpected fluctuations in production or sales, and "work in progress." According to the 1993 SNA, net acquisitions of valuables are also considered capital formation

External balance on goods and services (% of GDP) (Col. 10): External balance on goods and services (formerly resource balance) equals exports of goods and services minus imports of goods and services (previously nonfactor services).

CAPITAL COEFFICIENT (Col. 11): the ratio of the value of capital (ΔI) to the value of output (ΔGDP)

Foreign direct investment, net inflows (% of GDP) (Col. 13): Foreign direct investment are the net inflows of investment to acquire a lasting management interest (10 percent or more of voting stock) in an enterprise operating in an economy other than that of the investor. It is the sum of equity capital, reinvestment of earnings, other long-term capital, and short-term capital as shown in the balance of payments. This series shows net inflows (new investment inflows less disinvestment) in the reporting economy from foreign investors, and is divided by GDP.